A Day of Humanity

A Day of Humanity

Brady Bove

NEW DEGREE PRESS

A DAY OF HUMANITY

ISBN   978-1-64137-915-1 *Paperback*
        978-1-64137-671-6 *Kindle Ebook*
        978-1-64137-673-0 *Ebook*

For all that connects us

TABLE OF CONTENTS

NOTE FROM
THE AUTHOR

———

"Try to understand men. If you understand each other, you will be kind to each other. Knowing a man well never leads to hate and almost always leads to love."

JOHN STEINBECK

The idea for this book was born out of a two-hour discussion with my friend, Jesse Franklin. He managed to help me identify a passion of mine that had yet to see the light: the importance of human interaction. Without even realizing it, I'd been storing amazing interactions in my heart, those that I have experienced and some I've merely witnessed. For example, when I was out running one day, I experienced a mental shift. I went from feeling excited about the beauty of the day and the people I was passing to anxiety about my weekend and all the things I needed to do. While I barely registered this change, a couple of women noticed my altered expression and called me out on it, urging me to look outside my own mind and refocus on what I had appreciated so much before. That one, small interaction changed my entire outlook that day. During our conversation, Jesse encouraged me to open the storage closet in my heart and pull out these stories. Once I did, I realized I had to write about how I truly believe it is our interactions—with ourselves, with others, and with the world—that make us human. There is beauty in humanity—a beauty in knowing and being known.

Within the pages of this book, you will find a collection of stories. A few are based on my own experiences, but the majority are about the lives of incredible people. These people opened up and described their favorite, most meaningful, or simply random moments with me. Every story included in this book resonated with me on some level, and I hope that you, too, will find a connection here.

Some of the stories I share may express some opinions that you do not agree with. This book is not meant to be polarizing, but rather uniting. Even in our differences, so many of us feel similar emotions or face similar situations. It is these similarities and connections I wanted to illustrate in these stories, and I hope you can take something away from these connections.

We all strive to feel connected in life. With the rise of social media, we are more "connected" than ever, yet around half of Americans still feel lonely.[1] Even in our hyper-connected society, it is so easy to feel like the odd man out. It often seems every person we encounter is so different from us— that there are more things that separate us from each other than connect us. But if we go through life focusing on these differences, these separations, then we miss out on knowing and being known, two needs that we all carry in our hearts. As John Steinbeck wrote about—and as I've learned in the making of this book—to know is to love.

In the end, we are all so much more the same than we are different. We are all trying in life, and every moment is an interaction with each other and with the world. We are all

---

1   Polack, Ellie. "New Cigna Study Reveals Loneliness at Epidemic Levels in America." *Cigna.* May 1, 2018.

under the same sunrise, sky, and sunset. That's why I chose to walk through the timeline of a day to show you how we can all connect with each other in our daily lives, whether in a chance meeting on the subway, through caring for loved ones, through moments so embarrassing we want to hide, or surprisingly intimate moments shared with near strangers. The sections in this book are separated simply by the time they have occurred to show that as we move through our mornings, days, and nights, we are all connected.

Poetry is one way I interact with the world, and because of that connection, I wanted to showcase all of these stories in the best way I know how. I was once told that the best writing is that which affects the author in some way, and with the combination of powerful stories and the life raft that is poetry, I can promise that writing this book has moved me. By reading this book, I hope you can take away a greater appreciation for your journey through life, for others, and are reminded that, no matter what, you are not alone.

Before sharing with all of you the many wonderful stories I've collected, I want to begin by sharing one of my own. This poem represents one of the ways I interact with the world and why I consider poetry to be a life raft that helps keep me afloat.

My Love Poem to Poetry

When I was a kid,
engulfed in swirling anxiety,
depression knocked on my bedroom door.
These emotions tumbled inside,
played on water slides,
shot tears out of my eyes.
The psychologist helped me,
but only one thing saved me:
my discovery of poetry.

Sarah Kay was my role model.
The words danced from her mouth,
frolicked with the emotions in my brain,
yet listening and reading couldn't stop
the storm trembling within me.

A pen found my hand,
paper fluttered before me
urging me to write something.
Most kids have journals, but I had poetry.
My mind could wander, my mind could be free.
Finally, I found a peaceful land of liberty.

The words flowed from me, and
Sarah Kay still inspired me,
but she was no longer alone
in the kingdom of mighty poets.
I found Frost and E.H.,
and so many more that changed my world.
Of "the two roads diverged in a yellow wood,"[2]
I took the one

---

2   Frost, Robert. "The Road Not Taken." Poetry Foundation, accessed on
     June 1, 2020..

away from the war with my mind,
the one that freed my soul
one stanza at a time.
Poetry doesn't define me,
but it influences my feelings,
and how I view the spinning globe of reality
dressed in a blue and green gown
of human mortality.

Poetry is the string
that saves the balloon
from flying away in the sky,
and the balloon is really my mind,
seeking knowledge outside my world,
striving to better my life one lesson at a time.
Mistakes and memories are two ways
the balloon traveled high,
taught me the marvelous things
that dwell in the sky.

I explore the earth, for I'm not sure
where my future lies,
but poetry helps me figure out my mind,
and digest the knowledge that dwells inside.

I'd like to say I'm good enough
to maybe one day save a lost soul,
but today I write for myself
to understand the world.

Poetry is my hero and to know
me you must know:
my heart is writing perpetually,
and the words will never cease to flow.

MORNING

——

Sweet Smiles

The stranger walked:
    head down.
Focused on his trudging feet:
    a shadow to the world around.

She smiled to the stranger:
    so simple, so sweet.
The stranger smiled back:
    so joyful, so pleased.

The stranger smiled:
    a sunrise burst in his heart.
The whole way home:
    flowers blossomed in his soul.

Worries faded:
    happiness flowed freely.
Before he was scared:
    of reaching out, living life, messing up.

Her smile halted his fear:
    his head no longer down in dread.
For the first time he saw the world:
    smiles, beautiful people everywhere.

One Second

She had sparkly nails;
her students noticed.

Before talking physics,
they bonded over cosmetics.

Based off a story shared with author by Amanda Foutch

Prepare to Progress

Prepare

UT Pharmacy is my current dream.
    As I drive to finish my Bachelor's,
        I nervously apply early action, scared
            I won't stand out. *Am I good enough?*

They have me write a personal statement:
    all I've done, all I've thought, all of me.
        Temptation draws me in to say what they want to hear,
            I fight instead to say who I really am.

I feel confidence in <u>me</u>,
    like this passion, this dream, is possible.
        The week before the interview,
            my roommate builds me up, helps me feel calm.

She tells me I deserve this.
    That I'll kill it.
        I'm ready, indeed.

to

The interview is split into three sections:
    One. Micro-interviewing with a panel.
        Two. Building with toys while someone guides you.
            Three. Giving a pitch on "Why Pharmacy?"

In the first, my experience pays off,
    it's not that bad, I answer well.
        In the second, it's more fun than stressful,
            I interact with new people.

It's the third that makes me nervous,
I don't have time to prepare answers,
I don't get to introduce myself,
to relax and get a feel for the crowd.

In my group, I am the last to do it,
afterwards, I feel
good, confident!

Progress

For the rest of the day I am f l o a t i n g.

During the presentations, I listen to the
info for future students—*me(?)* I feel
like I killed it. *I will get in!*

As I leave, the weather is as wonderful
as I feel. I pick up my phone and
call my mother, "The interview
went great. I love it here!"

Early action is the right decision. I feel so
confident in my passions. It's hard to be
proud of myself sometimes, but
after this, I take time to feel it.

How great it is, to be on the right path
and know you are your best self.
P.S. I get in .

Based off a story shared with author by Kendra Rider

Just Tri

I float through the swim,
the run will be fun.
I'm still in shape
from high school teams.
400 yards toward success.
The five of us,
a brand-new team,
learn to shift bicycles
we've never ridden before—
loaners from Purdue.

Six miles in and
I'm dying.
Me, age eighteen,
huffing like Caesar
in that Roman tragedy,
Et Tu Bikus?
Men (and women) in their seventies
blowing by me.
Are my tires flat?
Nope, just my legs.
Am I going to make it back?
The run comes—
I'm decent,
but so tired.
Seventies come back in sight.
Maybe I'm doing alright.
Finish line.
Never again,
no more triathlons.

23

A month later, I'm back
in the pool,
starting another race.
Maybe I'm a fool, but
I'd hate myself if I didn't try,
this crazy dream of mine,
now part of my identity.

A few years pass,
the biggest race of my life—
an Ironman.
My legs may be dead,
but my resolve is alive.
There's not much better in life
than the will to tri.

Based off a story shared with author by Alexander Alvarez

Tennessee's Aubrey, Not Kansas' Dorothy

1:30AM
Just past the foothills,
in the heart of Tennessee,
the wind stops whistling—
its song no longer a peaceful melody,
now screaming like an injured chimpanzee
as it barrels and bounces off buildings
sheltering families.

No, we aren't in Kansas anymore—
the tornado doesn't drop the house
on an evil witch.
Instead, the house collapses
exhausted, the straw hut of the little pig
no match for the huffing of the big,
bad Mother Nature.
Aubrey and her family, losing everything.
Fear, deafening.
Hearts, pounding
in tune with the wind's screaming.

The crunching of metal joins the
wind's cacophony:
cars flip
and telephone poles fall
and Dorothy's red shoes
are nowhere to be found.
Even the sun hides
from the destruction that
unfolds,
as metal merges with falling trees.
The sun is too scared to shine
on this tragedy.

25

7:00 AM
But the sun must shine,
the storm ends
and people emerge from fallen homes.
Like Plato's cave people,
they see the world for the first time:
damaged homes and windblown dreams.

Aubrey addresses the sun head-on,
neither one to hide in the dark for long.
She steps outside into the light
without fear, with hope that all
can be rebuilt.
And as she walks,
a flare of blue dances
in the humming sunlight,
and she realizes that the tornado
didn't,
couldn't,
wouldn't
take everything away.
Her prom dress sways,
a little muddy, but still so pretty,
ready to be worn.
Even Dorothy couldn't shine as bright
in her own dress, blue and white—
this is Aubrey's show.

Aubrey's smile radiates
so no one can hide
in the darkness of rubble anymore.
Tennessee is hit hard,
but Aubrey, her blue dress,
and the yellow sun show the state
what it means to never let go
of hope.

Beres, Nick. "IN THE FACE OF SUCH DEVASTATION ... AND, THE LOSS OF 25 LIVES YOU TRY TO LOOK FOR SMALL SILVER LININGS," Facebook, Last Modified March 3, 2020.

A Movie in Central Park

The Opening Scene
In Central Park,
a mom and her daughter
walk close,
extras play and chat and walk
in the background, blurred.

Another woman comes in focus,
a friend.
The mom sees her,
they begin talking and talking
(the end doesn't seem near.)
The daughter, at first close by,
until something
catches her eye—
something red,
like a balloon, floating,
taunting, drawing her in.

The daughter is now curious
(as little children usually are).
She can't see what it is,
the mysterious red object
just out of focus,
but she needs to know.
So, she looks at her mom,
focuses in on her mouth,
talking and talking.
She decides to go.

27

Building to the Climax

Through Central Park,
the little girl walks alone.
Again, the extras flicker,
filler across the background.

She gets closer
and
closer,
and finally,
in disappointment she sees,
as the red thing comes in focus,
it is just a red scaffolding—
nothing.

Climax

In dismay she spins around,
scaffolding flying out of view,
it is nothing, still.
It is time she finds her mom.
Through the park, the flying frisbees,
the playing people, the extras
are the only things in focus.
Her mom—not even five feet tall—
doesn't stand out in the crowd.

This is a stop-motion animation;
every person walking past this little girl,
a flicker in her blurred vision
(she doesn't know she needs glasses.)
Legs flash in quick, impatient movements.

The focus on the girl,
breathing rapidly,
her eyes, center screen,
brimming with tears.

Full view, she is alone,
just her, with a blur of the extras,
all around, engulfing.

Denouement

A flicker of focus on red,
the scarf of her mom's friend.
The little girl's eyes enlarge.
She sees the woman
who had her mom's attention
locked in conversation.
Behind the friend,
another woman comes in view,
stepping out from the sea of extras—
the mom.

The extras spin out of view,
spotlight on the little girl
with tears (of joy)
streaming down her cheeks,
kisses from her mother
brush them away.

Based off a story shared with author by Olga Repp

29

no hablo inglés

I am nervous this morning,
my first day of fourth grade,
my first day of school in the States,
and worst of all,
no hablo inglés.

My parents have work.
I walk alone, the fall wind
starting to pick up,
and worst of all,
no hablo inglés.

I won't learn in my classes,
my teachers won't understand me,
and no one will be my friend,
because worst of all,
no hablo inglés.

I arrive to school early.
The teacher walks me to my desk.
I sit in silence, head down, crying,
because worst of all,
no hablo inglés.

A tap on my shoulder,
I look up sniffling.
A kid is there, says his name's Ricky,
he doesn't care at all,
no hablo inglés.

Author's Note: Ricky and Alex are still friends.

——————————————————

Based off a story shared with author by Alexander Alvarez

Waterfall

Paralyzed,
the whole world stopped spinning.
I was falling down a waterfall
but when water crashed into river,
I just kept falling
   and falling
    and f
      a
       l
        l
        i
         n
          g
          .

My brain on its own game show:
whoever thinks up the worst-case scenario
WINS!
Wins what?
A trip down the waterfall.

One morning, I hit bottom.
No more falling,
hard as rock.

At seventeen,
I didn't trust myself,
I didn't trust my God,
I didn't trust this world.
But first, I sat in Sunday School,
in blissful ignorance of my
stubbornness, my lack of reliance,
my phone on silent,
face down.

31

I knew Mom was in pain,
but she was going to the doctor today.

Mom activated Find My iPhone.
At first I was confused—
the whole class turned to look
as I slowly faced my phone,
the fear registering.
So many missed texts and calls,
all from Mom.
She needed to be driven to the ER.
All I could think, "this is it—"
my brain couldn't win the game today,
life already made worse
come to worst.

Maybe she had a terminal illness,
              needed surgery,
                    what if she was d
                            y
                           i
                              n
                                g
                               ?

The tears began to roll,
their own waterfall.
Without a word, I ran out,
sped home, ran through what I'd say
if a cop pulled me over,
words falling out of my mouth,
pleading, *Officer, let me go.*
I could barely see the road,
tears vying for control.
I tried to push them back,
I thought about Mom,
I needed to be strong.

I picked her up and off we drove.

In the emergency room,
my mom and her doctor were calm,
I was in the corner,
unable to contain my sobs.
They reassured me,
she'll be okay,
just an infection
from an earring she wore one day.
They seemed confused
that this visit was enough
to set me off.
They had no idea
the fears that were building,
paralyzing,
my falling down the waterfall.

I guess I lied.
Life didn't win the game,
it never would if I kept living this way.
Something I thought was normal—
always thinking of the worst-case scenario—
was actually something I could work on
and grow through,
no need to allow myself to

        f

      a

    l

    l

     .

Based off a story shared with author by Healey Sample

~~Dis~~Abilities

Their singing, more beautiful
than anything,
sun shining through the rain of life.
Their voices, colors on a rainbow,
more beautiful than any retouched photo
that makes colors brighter,
shadows lighter.
They are real, raw.
Their voices imperfect,
their pitches a little crooked,
but that's what makes them beautiful.

This masterpiece concludes a powerful week.
A week for those with disabilities
to feel at home,
to not worry about *can* or *can't*,
but to do all
through love.
Each time I leave with a lesson
on what it means to love,
to come together,
to look past our differences.
Through them I know
that perfect creation
comes with flaws,
and perfect love can be shared
in a song.

Based off a story shared with author by Lauren Brooke Massongill

7 Days and a Plane Ride

July 2, 2018, 7AM
I'm nervous,
goosebumps cover my arms.
My first time alone on a plane.

I'm not alone,
my twin sister comes,
but our parents aren't with us.

It's a big step for a girl
scared of heights
who hates when her ears pop.

I'm one of five—
there is no finding myself,
no individual identity.

We stick together,
that's what family is for.
This trip won't change a thing.

Seven days to learn
about economics in Ohio
with practical strangers—

I'll go back home
to little Delaware,
and life will be the same.

Back to high school,
to the same people
I've known forever,

to being a girl
in a small city, in a small state
whose life will never change,

to being a twin, to figuring out
what it means to be fifteen
in a big family.

July 8, 2018, 3PM
I sit here amazed, goosebumped,
my second time *almost* alone on a plane.
Seven days have changed me.

Seven days
with other upperclassmen,
former strangers with fiery passions

we shared as we discussed economics.
We built new connections, new skyscrapers of
education, innovation, creation.

I don't want to be stuck
in my little box of Delaware, in my little box
of Deborah. I can't stay in the box.

There's more than just me,
more than just me and my twin,
more than just us and our siblings.

I can be unstoppable—
not caring if my ears pop,
caring about being more than myself.

I don't know what all's out there,
but I'd bet everyday there's room to grow
and to change.

I look at the opportunity costs.
The costs of doing nothing
are too high to pay.

Based off a story shared with author by Deborah Olatunji

Family

My left hand is encased by the warm,
soft hand of my mother,
her touch light, loving.

Our fingers rest on the left hand of my father,
rough from dry skin and crazy weather.
My right hand wraps around his wrist.

| I've built a fort |
| out of their arms, their love. |
| Here I feel strong; |
| here I feel safe… |
| anything the world throws, |
| the three of us can take. |

People, Too

Should we tell kids the news?
The stories of death and division?
How long until we change their worldview?
Sometimes bad things happen, too.

She felt so much horror at the news report,
knowing the boy she babysat
was watching next to her,
leaning on her heart.

She tried to change the subject,
to focus on a game, a story,
something different,
something—anything—kid-worthy.

But this little boy, he already knew
the border was an area of dispute,
and it made him confused:
After all, he thought, *Mexicans are people, too.*

His innocence shielded him,
she could sigh in relief, he was ignorant
to deep-seated, partisan agony.
All he wanted was for the world to be happy.

Maybe she could learn from this little boy—
his youthful choice of harmony
over the divisiveness of adulthood.
Maybe we should all let our inner child out.

Based off a story shared with author by Alex Scearce

The Flight of a Lifetime

For one month,
  I woke at six AM,
    a baby bird stretching its wings,
     exploring this new world.
      Every morning we trained,
       every afternoon we worked out,
        practicing, *ready to catch a worm.*
      At night, we gave our coaches our phones—
       no distractions, *no other birds.*

      We took a train to Bangkok,
       to the National Team Training Facility,
      we trained even harder,
       our feathers fuller.
      We flew to China to try to qualify for the World Cup,
       our migratory flight left us hungry for a win.

        We shared meals with the teams from
        South Korea,
        Iran,
        North Korea,
         their feathers shone with different colors,
         their chirps a different rhythm.
        We knew we would play them,
         but our interest in each other was greater
         than our enmity on the field.
        If only for a night,
         our differences aside,
         our voices combined,
         a beautiful symphony of song.

When we competed against North Korea,
I was amazed
my coaches had me play.
Each game only had three substitutions,
and here I was,
flitting my wings on the sidelines,
playing on a national level.
I was so nervous;
I was shaking.
All my preparation,
my whole life,
building up to this moment.
Could I catch a worm?
Was I good enough?

Our competitors were big and fast,
their fierce wings creating shadows over us
as they flew.
I was distracted,
excited,
incredibly nervous.

At first, I was disappointed,
I didn't play as well as I wanted,
but it was my first time on the field,
my first time flying high.
We might not have won,
I might not have caught a worm,
but I'm proud of myself.
I know I did my best then,
and if I could do it again, I'd be ready.
That's enough to make me happy.

That field made me free.
Even if I'm never on the national stage again,
I know that the lessons I learned,
the memories I hold,
the relationships I formed,
are enough to feed my soul,
and that is so much better than a worm.

Based off a story shared with author by Jen Ternullo

The Wisdom of Youth

Adriana
was lost in the crowd—
so focused on comparing
she kept putting herself down,
worrying she wasn't enough,
letting her individuality drown.

One morning,
her sister approached,
sat her down
and began her loving reproach.
I see what you're doing. This isn't YOU.
Here are some tips, sister, I love you.

Adriana's little sister, only eleven,
when most pre-teens
were focused on
their body changing,
trying to fit in,
she wasn't afraid to be herself.

Adriana was inspired,
her younger sister, wiser
than those three times her age.
In Adriana, a spark,
a transformation,
a journey to self-identification.

Adriana vowed to become
unapologetically
true.

Based off a story shared with author by Adriana Conte

43

An Irish Family Reunion

Son

As the mother of two boys,
I am used to chaos and noise:
things breaking, kids playing, toys rolling.

It was quiet on Saint Patrick's morning.
Rob in his room, Chris, outside playing.
Peace, until the phone started ringing,

The quiet shattered by a boy screaming
about how Chris had fallen, cut his knee, blood gushing.
He was in the ER, no time to stall!

In the hospital for my dear son,
I turned the corner, I run
past half-opened curtains, in there, my grandmother!

Grandma

In her 90s, Grandma loved her brandy,
she always seemed to have a bottle handy,
discreetly, daintily sipping her drink.

That morning, she had a fall,
my mother was called,
off they went to the ER, no time to stall!

The doctor entered her room,
politely asked if she drank before noon.
She said she didn't have any brandy.

After completing the blood test,
they told my grandma she had to rest,
because she was dizzy from being tipsy.

Catering Trays

Mini Tray
Feeds +/- 6 People
Italian & Home Style Turkey Breast & American Cheese

Assorted Tray
Feeds +/- 10 People
Italian & Home Style Turkey Breast & American Cheese, Ham & American Cheese

Deluxe Tray
Feeds +/- 14 People
Two Italians, Home Style Turkey Breast & American Cheese, Ham & Cheese

Super Deluxe Tray
Feeds +/- 20 People
Two Italians, Roast Beef & American Cheese, Home Style Turkey Breast & American Cheese, Ham & Cheese

Super Duper Deluxe Tray
Feeds +/- 25 People
Two Italians, Home Style Turkey Breast & American Cheese, Ham & American Cheese, Roast Beef & American Cheese, Nonna's Veggie

Italian Sampler
Marinated Mozzarella, Pepperoni Bites, Sharp Provolone, Roasted Red Peppers, Olive Shooters, Buffalo Cheese Bites & Sopressata

Pepperoni & Cheese Sampler
Pepperoni & Sharp Provolone

Cheese Sampler
Imported & Domestic Cheese

Pre-Order Your Trays Today!

843.606.2636 • Full Menu Visit PrimoHoagies.com

OLD FASHIONED STYLE
PrimoHoagies & Steaks
ITALIAN SPECIALTY SANDWICHES

NOT A REWARDS MEMBER?
Join now at primohoagies.com/rewards or text **"PRIMO"** to 484-270-4000

I left to check on my son, instead,
passing another row of hospital beds,
and sitting there was my cousin, with a crooked stare.

Cousin

Her hand over her eye,
like she had gotten in a fist fight.
She just hit her face.

They looked at her cornea
to check her sight after the trauma.
Luckily, she'd be okay.

What a crazy reunion for a very Irish family.
I just wonder what the doctors were thinking
when we all stumbled in on that very Irish holiday.

Based off a story shared with author by Patricia Bove

The Bully, Part 1

Ten-year-old boys, thinking they own the world,
loud and rowdy, forgetting the hour,
school about to begin.
Then comes teacher, teeth glistening.
Did she get them whitened again?

She calls the class to attention,
Ten-year-old boys, wiggling in their seats.
Jack's got a new hoodie, Charlie a stain on his knee.
Alex's in the back, noticing everything.
Is the teacher about to speak?

There's to be a new student—Zach Hardy!
Hardy, like the series Alex likes to read.
He runs to the shelf, holds up a book
triumphant like a trophy, sleuths by the same name.
Will it smell as sweet?

With one eye peeking around the door frame,
there's a new ten-year-old boy.
He looks a little strange, but it's too early to say.
"This is Zachary, boys, **be nice.**"
Will they be friends?

Based off a story shared with author by J. A. Muñoz

The Sunny Cat

Meow
A kitten peeked
around the corner
like the sun peeked
above the horizon,
patient,
slow,
alerting me
to the coming day.
Something big would happen.
I knew the kitten wasn't it as
its tags glinted in morning sun.

I sighed.

I picked up the orange cat,
made more orange
in the yellow beams of light.
My knees buckled from his weight—
at only eight,
I wasn't as strong as my love for kittens.
I crossed the street,
leaving Grandfather's house in shadow.

Meow
the cat sang in appreciation as
I attempted to lift my arms a little higher
returning him to his master,
another little girl named Kasey.

Kasey lived in the house with big windows—
the kind that let in the sun,
no questions asked.

47

She opened their yellow door wider,
just enough to let me and the sun inside.
Her invitation to play
warmed me more than those rays.
I loved to play Barbie in her room,
the one that faced east and the morning sun.
For a whole week, every morning,
we'd imagine.

Until the clouds came,
the visit to Grandfather's ended
and I had to go back home,
leaving Grandfather's house in shadow.

Meow
The orange cat greeted me with a familiar gleam.
It had been a couple of years,
but I knew he remembered.
My grandfather needed someone to care for him,
his nights were getting longer.
So we left Florida,
and stayed with him from then on.

The cat signaled
across the street
to the wide windows and yellow doors,
to the house with a sunshine warmth
even in its darker corners.
To Kasey.

Meow
Over the years, Kasey and I stayed close,
grew closer,
watched the sunrise
as we studied, or sang,

or did whatever
teenage girls dreamed of.
Thirty-six years later,
our friendship could never be stronger.
She knows me better than anyone,
better than the sun knows the sky,
its light changing our lives.

With Kasey around,
even after I moved out,
no shadow could touch my grandfather's house.

Meow.

Based off a story shared with author by Kelly Pfender Clark

It Gets Better

In a white coat,
his stethoscope shines.
Until now,
I've only told him lies—
I'm fine, I'm fine,
there's nothing else wrong
with my mind.

But then last night,
the pain came.
Today, exhaustion rang,
became a sorry friend
to self-hatred
for letting myself go
until almost too late.

Now, it *has* to get better;
I have to make a change.
Every question he asks,
I'll answer, despite the malaise.
"Do you feel useless?"
Often, and then I force myself
to do something, refuse to rest.

"And how about anxious?"
Ever since I can remember.
Even on good days, I lose
my breath and shake,
obsessed with finding the root:
something to be the reason.

I want to, need to
get better,
please help,
doctor.

...

Epilogue
Three months later and
medication has turned my life around.
I work on my rationalization,
taking responsibility for my actions,
and accepting all of me,
even my anxiety and depression.

Based off a story shared with author by Haley Newlin

51

DAY

Smile Miss

Souris mademoiselle!
The aches of my body
seem to lift with my smile,
a full one, not limited
by how fast I can run the mile,
or how heavy my body feels,
powered only by the positivity
passed between me and
two beautiful women
who happen to wear an outward sign
of their religion,
but who most importantly are people,
sharing joy with me.

I've been running around the lake
as the midday sun bounces
from the water to dance across
the wings of ducks.
The trees sing, bright green,
in the heat of a French summer.
I follow the stream
of walkers, skaters, and players.
Circling the lake like a clock,
I'm the second hand,
lap after lap,
two miles.
I turn to reverse the route,
each person I pass,
our eyes meet,
I try to smile sweet,
But my legs heave
with each minute.
The clock I'm running

55

is slowly ticking,
the trees' song turns sour,
sickly green,
the sun pushes light
into my eyes,
blinding.
Lap after lap,
another mile.
I forget to fake a smile.

These women
have seen each lap,
returned each smile,
each mile,
and when I fail to react,
they yell
Souris mademoiselle!
I turn my head.
I don't speak French, but
I know exactly what they mean
from high school Spanish?
Divine Providence?
It doesn't matter how,
their message helps me see
past my run
and achy knees,
past my worries
and anxieties,
to the trees' melody
and the sunshine's shimmer,
to this second,
this opportunity.

Smiling with strangers
of different countries,

languages, religions, ages,
who I will never see again,
who now mean
something very special to me.

If Time Is an Ocean

We like to say we've been friends forever,
before we entered this world,
destined to be together.
Our moms, best friends,
in each other's weddings,
didn't give us the opportunity to choose.
We met when we were barely two.
Though we lived an hour apart,
we stuck together.

But then at ten, she moved to Texas.
We had no cell phones—
like Israelites facing the Red Sea,
no boat to carry us free.
How would our friendship fare
between the crashing waves of time
and the distance of sand?
We needed paper and a bottle
to cast our notes to the ocean,
let the tide of time carry
stories of our separate lives,
and dreams of the day
we would reunite.

As we aged,
we moved to text,
Instagram, Snapchat,
bigger bottles, longer notes.
With every visit,
without fail, every time we talked,
it was like we never stopped.
If time is an ocean,
our friendship is Moses,
parting the sea.

The Bully, Part 2

It must have rained;
the dark mud begins to stain
as they wrestle on the playground
underneath swaying swings,
Alex holds his football with an iron grip.

He brought his ball to share,
but when they split up into teams,
the ten-year-old captains chose
until they left him standing there, the spare.
They took his ball from him.

Alex scurries to the field,
and hears the words that change his day:
"You can't play."
He turns to Zach, mouth agape.
Alex grabs his ball, begins to walk away.

Zach pushes him to the ground!
Everyone gathers around,
as two ten-year-old boys
squirm in the mud.
The rude vs. the excluded.

Alex thinks he's earned the right to play,
but as time passes, he stands alone.
At least now he knows,
that it matters how you act:
the bullies don't always win.

Based off a story shared with author by J. A. Muñoz

Why I Hate Ice Cream Trucks But Love my Parents

When I was a kid,
we lived in a tenement,
in inner-city Boston.
Five kids and two parents
who never went to college.
We didn't have everything
but had *everything* we needed.

The ice cream truck would
bumble down the road,
its siren call causing kids to drop toys,
run to Mom or Dad and beg for coins.
But we didn't have the money,
so the truck would come and go,
its song echoing through our ears
down to our empty tummies.

But my mother had a solution,
she always did.
She cut the ice trays open, stuck
a spoon in the middle and
filled Kool Aid to the brim,
to help us cool off in the summer heat.
It may not have been the perfect treat,
but it was *perfect* for me.

Based off a story shared with author by Jerry Boyle

Nickie.

My first semester of law school
was a nightmare come true.
It was something brand new,
I tried my best to fit in.
Everyone seemed to be excelling.
I was struggling.

As the semester went on,
my friendships weren't strong.
Alone, isolated, I contemplated
dropping out, leaving,
doing something else completely,
my own provisional remedy.

But *I didn't come this far
just to come this far.*

...

With the end of first semester,
I hoped it would be better
if I became my loneliness' abettor.
It was close to the end of the year,
so I called these emotions "fear"
ignoring them as term paper deadlines
drew near.

One day I texted Nickie,
talking about something silly.
Afterwards she texted sincerely:
Are you okay?
You don't seem like yourself lately.
I'd been holding my emotions so tightly.
I found myself crying

because I wasn't alone.

61

...

I don't know how I got so lucky
to have Nickie
always looking out for me.
Her text was the first time
I didn't feel left behind.
I owe her my life.

I once read that
Loyalty is not something that simply happens.[3]
Nickie proves this
time and time again.
She's my attorney of life,
always at my defense.
She was there when I was drowning,
unafraid to swim along with me.

That is who she is,
my friend, Nickie.

---

3   Reilly, Matthew. Scarecrow: A Shane Schofield Thriller (London:
    ST. Martin's Press, 2004), 367.
    Based off a story shared with author by Zach Donahue
    "I didn't come this far just to come this far" is a direct quote from Zach

Lost

Tears amidst a crowd.
Don't cry little boy, don't cry!
Your mom will be found.

His Croatian skin
shines through the Italian throng.
But his mom is gone.

The leather shop man
comforts the boy as his friend
searches in the crowd.

Behold! Another
boy, panting, his brother found.
The crowd claps in joy.

This bustling market,
no match for brotherly love—
together again.

Fear Parks

The air is full of electricity
humming with joyful screams,
saturated with a symphony of aromas—
of motor oil, funnel cakes, and sweat,
pushed to the side by massive rides
speeding past,
taking my breath as I watch.

I feel my fear
    bubble to the surface,
    run laps in my stomach,
    climb my throat like a rock wall,
    seep from my pores like whack-a-mole.
Nope, never. Roller coasters are my nemesis.

The five people I've come with—
practically strangers,
we met at camp this weekend—
urge me to ride one,
motivate me like I'm running a marathon.
My heart is beating so fast,
maybe I am.
If I die,
tell my mom it's your fault.
I take a leap of faith into the rollercoaster cart.

What kind of name is GateKeeper anyways?
The harnesses click click click,
and the whole world turns upside down.
If I survive this, I'm going to kill you!
Maybe that's the fear talking—
it's already taken control of my lungs,
why not take my voice?
And so I scream.

I scream as the ride
forces my body faster and faster,
upside down again and again.
When will this torture end?
Two minutes later, a jolt,
a stop,
I hear my scream
flying down the track for round two,
but my body doesn't move.

My breath, my voice, my stomach, my skin, my throat—
it's all there, it's all mine, it's all safe and sound.
The fear is nowhere to be found (for now)!
I could even do it again (for now)!

I rode the GateKeeper at Cedar Point,
and I didn't—I couldn't—do it alone.
With help, I really can do
anything I set my mind to.

Based off a story shared with author by Deborah Olatunji

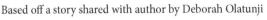

65

Kite Strings

I am passing fields of flowers,
yellow and purple meld together
as the train speeds past.
In the meadows I am following
with my soul on a kite string
billowing in the excitement of
the destination to come.
Up in the clouds,
I'm lost in my mind,
until two toddlers bring me down,
pull my kite string back to the now.

They both are with their families,
waddling down the aisle
toward the other.
The family before me,
blue eyes, blonde hair,
and alluring Australian accents
moves to the back of the train.
The family behind,
perfect eyebrows, dark hair,
and calming Castillian cadences
sashays to the front.

The adults ignore the toddlers
because their languages
present a barrier,
but they know neither
and connect.
They smile and wave,
and tension dissipates.
This wall their parents built
melds into my kite string,

lifts into the air,
and we are all present,
connected by
two toddlers
who know only the language of love.

Based off a story shared with author by Alex Scearce

More than a Career

My career is not my life.
It is not all I am.
But I cannot lie,
it feeds so many other parts,
like the top of a fountain
giving its all
to every pool below.
Nursing helps me value
every moment, big and small:
Seeing my husband walk down the aisle.
Learning from my patients about life,
*   new and old.*
It's all connected,
and it's all connected to me.

A Dream Come True

So many young girls dream
about their wedding,
their groom, Prince Charming—
I was no exception.
I'd have a white dress,
family and friends there,
of course.

And now it's here.
The white dress no longer
a dream,
but a silky, soft reality,
obscured by my veil.
The church doors loom before me,
nerves bouncing in my brain,
more than my little cousin
playing with the flowers.

"Are you cold?" I ask her.
"Do you need to go inside?"
For a second,
I needed to care for her
to take care of myself.

I take deep breaths
to hold onto these emotions—
excitement and nervousness,
a cocktail I've never had before.
A moment I've waited my whole life for.
A moment I'll never have again.
A moment rooted in the promise
to care for one another.

So Precious

This baby in my arms,
barely 20 weeks old,
born 20 weeks early.
Her surrounding tubes
form a blanket of plastic.
Sensors beep throughout the room,
her own sound machine
for an atypical nursery.

Even before birth,
her life was hard:
a mother addicted to drugs,
no stable home.
But a baby needs touch,
and how blessed am I
to love something so precious.
Nursing gives me
this amazing moment,
this baby in my arms—
this real love.

69

To Be Naked

Her body is failing.

At first, barely here,
the coma held her captive,
but when it released its hold
she told stories of her life—
teaching in third world countries,
speaking eight languages.
If the coma's cage hadn't weakened
from our pleading, the medication,
I would never have known.

And now, her decision—
stay in the hospital,
and live by machine,
sick until the end,
or move to hospice,
where in six months
she would leave this earth.

Her family begs her to stay.
But she knows what she wants—
to be naked when she dies:
no tubes, no IV, no lines.

She can spend her final days
with her family,
free to be
happy, to laugh, to die.
She has a peace I've never seen.
She teaches me to accept
the things
we all have
in common—

the beauty of
a good life
and a good death.

Based off a story shared with author by Maggie R.

A Special Encounter

One day,
one encounter,
one Sunday,
my life changed forever,
my relationships grew fuller,
my loneliness skulked in the corner.

Every friendship
had rested on the surface
on purpose.
With everyone at a distance,
they would remain
ignorant to
my pain,
my suffering,
my depression.

It was my 20th birthday and
I couldn't go another decade
with this pain on my shoulders,
never close to another.

One day,
my birthday,
that Sunday,
I walked past a church
where my acquaintances prayed.

They were reading the Bible and
as they read,
the suffering of my heart
was written on pages
thousands of years old.

It was then I found my Lord.
And through my God, I found
friendships,
relationships fuller than
ever before.

I learned my suffering—
my pain—
was no longer a cage,
but a part of being human,
and then I knew
I never had been alone,
and never would be again.

My God,
my friendships,
one day,
one encounter,
this next decade
would be better.

Based off a story shared with author by E.H.

Pool Day with Pierson and Frankie

Frankie and Pierson practically
climb over each other
on the couch
as they prepare to tell me their story.
I sit patiently,
waiting to hear what silly thing
they got themselves into.
They begin their story,
I pick up my pen,
ready to take notes.

Pool Day.

Pierson (7 years old):
We are swimming.
The water isn't letting me breathe,
my friend is trying to help me
because he thinks Frankie
is drowneding me,
but we were just playing.
He's pushing her down,
but she's leaning on me
so I'm double drowneding.

Frankie (9 years old):
I wasn't drowning Pierson,
but his friend is choking me,
his hands on my neck,
it's hard to breathe.

Pierson:
I'm really scared
I'm gonna drowned.
I am nervous,

I'll never see my dad again.
Ruby [the dog] will miss me.
Where's Frankie?
I need to breathe,
I'm going to die,
I haven't hit a homerun yet,
I'm so scared.
Can someone help me?
I'm drowneding!

Frankie:
I know I'm not going to die.
Pierson's friend lets go,
we'll be fine.

It's okay.

Their story is of fear—
I was ready to hear
about childhood adventures:
fighting pirates,
making daisy chains,
playing tag in the rain.

We assume children are naive
to deep feelings—
knowledge of death, fear, despair—
but emotions don't discriminate
by age, and in fear,
things become clear.

Based off a story shared with author by Frankie and Pierson Gilbert

75

stage fright

He's in front of the podium.
Bright lights.
Eyes staring, unwavering.
It's time to begin his speech.
As people fill the auditorium's seats,
he sees his friends' encouraging smiles.

Deep inhale.

For a moment he is back in second grade—
he can't
breathe, sweat trickles down
his back, he has the
shakes.
Teacher gets the class to turn around—
it doesn't help, his heart still pounds.
She tries to get the class to leave
but he knows they're still listening.

Deep exhale.

There's no reason not to try.
Practice helped in high school—
two hundred students
isn't much more than twenty...
right?
It's time to begin,
competing for valedictorian,
only the best speech-giver wins.
He starts with gratitude:
it's his opportunity to express
how much the kindness
he received meant.
He thanks those who walked
with him each step.

Deep inhale.

His confidence is beginning to grow
like the beans they planted in second grade science.
How far he's come since then,
even Jack with his magical beanstalk would be amazed.

Deep exhale.

He moves on to
the importance of perseverance,
a topic that hits close to home for many in attendance.
He calls on those who he knows had tough moments,
who stayed and fought their battles.
"Life is a beautiful struggle."

Deep inhale.

He recalls his favorite movie as a child—
the lessons it taught him—
watching with his mouth slightly ajar,
popcorn sitting in his frozen hand
as she sang the famous song.

Deep exhale.

He longs to share the same wisdom with his classmates,
so he opens his mouth, slightly ajar, and begins,
not to talk in the magical whale language, but just to sing
about how important it is to never stop swimming.
He perfectly encapsulates the beautiful
struggle of life and the need for perseverance.
He has full control of himself: his breath, his heart, his sweats.

Deep inhale.

77

He looks up at the Two Hundred
and he smiles,
knowing that even if he doesn't win
the coveted position
of valedictorian,
he has won something better—
the knowledge that
skills can be learned,
     impacts can be made,
          fears can be conquered,
   if we jump in the ocean and
swim without stopping.
The auditorium breaks into applause.
His speech resonates
with the second grader
in each of their hearts.
And with that he bows graciously
and walks off the stage.

Deep exhale.

Based off a story shared with author by Godwin Chan
"Life is a beautiful struggle" is a direct quote from Godwin

"Welcome to Starbucks"

I never knew what friendship meant before.
Like a Starbucks drink, I let myself be poured
and poured and poured out
with no hope of being filled again.

In college, things changed when I met these girls—
from a black coffee to a latte with milk swirls.
When one of us was down (and sometimes just for fun),
we'd pile in a car, laugh and cry and sing at the top of our lungs.

In the drive-thru our conversations flourished
as Starbucks left our tummies nourished.
They poured themselves back into me,
loved me for my flaws and bitter drink.

Now we live in different cities,
so we get our drinks virtually,
FaceTime in the drive-thrus.
"Welcome to Starbucks," where friendship is true.

Based off a story shared with author by Emily Vander Bent

"You cry, because it's the human thing to do."

Three years ago—the last time I saw my best friend.
I remember in college thinking that time in our lives
would never end—even after graduation, I thought
our friendship would be the same, that
we'd see each other every weekend—
but that's not how life works.
I went to law school,
he joined the Peace Corps.
After Africa, he turned down Apple, Microsoft, Google
to stay and start an engineering firm,
to teach locals about self-sustaining farms.

Seven years ago, college freshmen,
we played rugby together,
and the pieces to friendship fell into place—
there was no need to start with the edges
and work your way in, hoping two pieces were matches.
By our last year, we were best friends.
He was the one I turned to first,
he was always there.

Three years ago, our last day together,
we sat at a Starbucks picnic table, worn down
from our friendship and the peaceful rays of the sun.
We sat for hours—other friends came and went—
talked about the path our friendship
had led us down.
And what is one to do before *goodbye*,
except to let go and cry?
You cry, I thought, *because it's the human thing to do.*
I cried because

I wouldn't be where I am without him,
I wouldn't be as good of a person or as strong.
I cried because
my friendship with him was a gift,
a blessing, **years** of life filled with goodness and fun.
I cried because
it would be our last day, and this picnic table would
never again see
our flavor of humanity.

Based off a story shared with author by Zach Donahue.
"You cry, because it's the human thing to do" is a direct quote from Zach.

How Many Years Has it Been?

How many years has it been
since you sneaked me on the college team
or further back, when we raced
for our high school teams?

How many years has it been
since you changed the course of my life
by inviting me that morning
to join you, me a little behind?

I remember you from high school:
doing what your brother had dreamed
until the accident forced him to stop.
You took it up—one of the nation's best.

We were off to West Virginia.
You, on scholarship—
they knew talent when they saw it—
me, a regular student—
who saw no talent in himself.

But then that morning, I saw you
running across the yard,
out for your morning "jog"—
a "casual" five miles.

Somehow, you remembered me—
just the kid you'd run laps
around when we would compete.
Nobody special, nobody fast.

I don't know how you remembered,
but you always were so nice to me.

I hated morning running, but I liked you,
so off we went.

And then, again, the next morning.
And again, again, again.

You told me to come to practice.
I looked at you like you were crazy,
but what else was I to do?
I didn't want to be lazy.

I joined you that morning—
ten miles straight from hell.
And though I hoped to die,
you convinced me to come again.

And then, again, the next morning.
And again, again, again.

Cross country ended, indoor track began.
"Why don't you race it?
It's no big commitment."
So I tried, wasn't too shabby,
and you invited me out again.

And then, again, the next morning.
And again, again, again.

The coach gave me a uniform—*no big
commitment yet*—but then I got shoes,
sweats, somehow made it on the roster.

And even though you left,
your legacy is real. Years later, I find
your email address from a college
where you coach a brand-new team.

I want you to know
that when you asked me to join you,
insignificant as it seemed,
you changed my life forever.

So, how many years has it been
since you got me to show up again,

and then, again, the next morning,
and again, again, again?

Based off a story shared with author by Kevin Stout

Kids Everywhere Hate Homework

Growing up in tenement houses,
with a bucket of coal
and furnace to heat us,
my room was always cold.
Then one day, my father came home,
his chest puffed, his eyes proud:
he was going to install a heater
of our own.
We would be warm from now on.
He pointed to us, the boys,
told us to take the heavy coal
to our neighbors.
They needed it now,
not us.
We did as we were told.

The first year,
my dad asked every morning,
how's the heat up there on the second floor?
is it keeping you toasty and warm?
And every morning we would say *yes*.
We slept like bears, the winter unable
to touch us in our dreams,
heated through hibernation.
Each morning our *yeses* made him
smile in satisfaction—
he did all he could
to bring some comfort to our lives.

The second year,
the heat wasn't so warm,
we needed extra blankets
as the winter entered our home.

85

My dad's eyes were less bright,
and every morning he would sigh.
Eventually, he called up the heating guy.

The expert came, climbed to the vent,
opened it up, and was left with a bump
on his head,
as books bounced off him and onto the bed!

My brother was stashing, avoiding
his homework and textbooks.
Sacrificing his warmth to prolong
the consequences of procrastination.

Based off a story shared with author by Jerry Boyle

"How's the Weather?"

Rho contained a joy
foreign to all but children
who haven't met sadness in life,
especially on bingo days.
It took practice to understand,
but then she'd get it and win the hand.
"Tell Daddy what I won, Brenda!"
she'd exclaim, forgetting the four dollars in her grip.

Some days they would sit on the small couch,
holding hands, discussing small nothings.
Rho knew that weather was a good topic
for when you don't know what to say:
"How about the weather? What do you think?"
Every few minutes she would repeat this,
Brenda answering the same every time.

Brenda would ask her if she wanted to
go outside of their little apartment,
play with friends or walk in the warm sun.
Rho would always answer the same way:
"No! Brenda, we cannot forget Daddy!"
So they would stay on the couch,
talking about the weather.

Brenda didn't know it would be so hard
to be a parent to her own mother—
the woman she talked to every day,
about everything, was now gone.
So Brenda would hold her hand and talk about rain.

Sometimes Brenda feels drained, missing her mom.
Her dad, too, with Parkinson's, is different.

She still loves them and would do it again.
She's glad her brother sacrifices to be the rock
for her parents full-time. Together, the three children try
to provide comfort,
but it's hard when these roles reverse.

Based off a story shared with author by Brenda Morris In Loving Memory of
Rhoda Kosoy

Diary of a Young Traveler:
The Best Day at Ha-Long Bay

The earth spins
tens of thousands
of miles each day,
but I can't feel it;
everything is still.
The world has stopped
here.

The warm sun dances
for my attention
between clouds
as cool wind
brushes my skin,
pulling me in.

The water,
a dichotomy:
cool and serene below us
while throwing
itself against rocks
on the other side of the bay.

It kisses the edge,
tossing the smell
of salt and oysters
towards our boat
like a kid skips stones.
The smells mingle
toward our noses.

All senses overflow
with my surroundings,

89

making the world feel still,
serene.
Everything around me
is right,
perfect.

My friends are by me,
sharing this moment,
soaking in this memory.
This world I am seeing
holds my future—
my career, my life—
but none of that matters.

We are lying on the water,
still,
as the world starts to spin.

Based off a story shared with author by Ching-Chi Tu

Love Letters

The letter is soft in my hand,
calming like the cool side of a pillow.
It reminds me of the comforts of home,
written with love that I pray
everyone gets a chance to know.
A love letter
for me, their humble teacher.
Their gratefulness runs off the paper
with black ink, carefully placed.
My life is full of grace.
The struggles have purpose,
because after so many years
of tears, I have found my niche—
These kids of broken homes,
disciplinary woes, lost hope.
I can't just be a teacher or a mentor,
I have to love them and form them.
And to do that,
I had to be formed in a forge.

I was eleven,
great at social studies and writing,
but couldn't pick up the slack in math.
I had tutors of all types and tried my best,
but teachers said, *because I'm a girl,*
I would never be good at math.
It was all my fault.

I was seventeen,
class secretary, loved cheerleading,
my friends going off to college,
and I wanted to follow suit,
but math brought my GPA down;
nothing I could do would turn it around.

91

And even though I did everything I could,
they wouldn't let me in—
the dim-witted, blonde cheerleader,
lonely and sad and dumb.

Never going to amount to much.
I was never going to reach my dream
of teaching.
But I couldn't give up yet.

I was nineteen,
finishing community college,
my math grade high enough
to get into a four-year institution.
I even made a D my sophomore year.
I was over the moon,
confidence swelling like a balloon,
maybe teaching was something I really could do.

Next semester,
stat class was a punch in the gut.
For every assignment, my roommate and I
would sit and work.
I'd struggle all day, every time,
just to fail.
It was brutal.
I felt the balloon begin to shrivel.
I wanted to take a new professor,
but he was also my advisor.
I had to take the same class
and attempt to pass.
I failed again.

I was called to his office,
he told me to abandon my dream,
statistics is necessary to be a teacher,

I would never be good enough.
It's the only thing I wanted to do,
but he didn't care,
and with a glassy stare,
said I'd be dropped from
the teaching program.

I felt my life was about to end.
Everything I had done—
all my hard work,
just to get to college
to pursue my dream—
gone.
They said I couldn't do
what I felt called to.

I was twenty-two,
about to graduate in psychology,
when a teacher took interest in me,
she identified a learning disability.
Dyscalculia.
All those years,
all the pain,
feeling like I would never be
good enough.
It wasn't my fault.
I had dyslexia for numbers;
equations were all jumbled.
My GPA bounced up,
I graduated, worked in a group home
helping kids with special needs.
It was a wonderful experience,
but not my dream.
I still desperately
wanted to teach.

93

I was a little older,
back to night school.
earning a teaching degree with
a GPA I could never have imagined (3.9),
the balloon billowing,
my life changing.

Now, nineteen years later,
this letter in my hand
shows me my struggle
meant something.
My journey had a purpose:
after all these years teaching,
I give kids the help I once needed.
I tell them
when someone says you can't
over and over again,
know that every minute spent
chasing your dreams will never be
spent in regret.
You're smart and you're good
and don't listen to them,
it's up to you to decide
what you can do.
I believe in you.

I open the letter and read
about that troubled child
who was told he would never do anything—
he now owns a business
and is truly excelling,
partly due to me, he says.
Then it's true—this letter shows,
my path of pain helped at least one man.
It's all worth it then.

———————————————————————

Based off a story shared with author by Sue Pezza

NIGHT

———

Be Our Guest

It all started with a knock on my door.
I'd just moved in.
I didn't know anyone on my floor,
so who could it be?
Two girls were waiting,
and then began insisting,
(even though I'd already eaten)
insisting I come join them.

We went to the kitchen,
where I met all their friends
sitting around a table of tajines and tea.
We were in France,
I was American,
they were Moroccan.
It was like they didn't see the difference.
I was just their friend, their guest.

I felt like Belle,
lost in the beauty of their spell
as they poured me tea,
gave me scrumptious things to eat.
I would be their guest.
Their conversation flowed
from French to Arabic,
I did my best to follow.

Out of my comfort zone,
and feeling so, so loved,
these strangers,
they went out of their way
to be kind.
For hours we laughed and talked,

left closer than I could've hoped, forged
friendships that would last
past any borders
between us.

Their friendship taught me
the value of other cultures,
the importance of discovering
what you didn't know before,
that a story can be formed with pages
from different books;
different girls from different worlds,
brought together
to learn, to grow,
to love, and to know
beauty is found
outside your comfort zone.

Based off a story shared with author by Maggie May

Wrinkly Skin

The oldest of four
at eight,
I should get to stay up late
to see Grandma, to jump up and hug her,
as she walks through the door,
stepping over toys on the floor.

I don't want to have to wait,
to just fall into her arms.
My grandma, she has that charm
that makes you feel so loved,
like nothing bad can happen
'cause she'll do all she can to stop it.

I wanna be like Grandma,
fun and brave and strong—
things I always seem to do wrong.
So tonight, I wanna stay up late.
To show her how much I love her,
I know I can stay up, I'm sure.

But my parents send me off to bed,
with the promise of Grandma's kiss
to send me off in a dreamy bliss
if I'm not already asleep
(which they think I will be).
I can stay up, I'll be sneaky.

...

Soft skin,
with wrinkles beginning to form,
her cheek against my cheek, so warm,

99

what a wonderful dream.
I didn't mean to fall asleep,
I even refused to count sheep.

I guess I wasn't strong enough.
Grandma would've been able to stay awake,
just add it to my long list of mistakes.
Am I worthy of her love?
At least, in my sleep, she's here,
and it feels so sincere.

So real.
Is it? Could it be?
My eyes open, blurry,
to a set of loving eyes.
I touch her wrinkly skin and see
Grandma is here with me.

I'm so happy.
Grandma is here for a goodnight kiss,
my mom kept her promise.
I feel so special, so loved.
This is better than any dream.
This is my favorite memory.

———————————————————————

Based off a story shared with author by Maria Rosa Muñoz

The Five Stages

Ye Ye is my grandfather
and my role model
and my best friend.
In Chinese culture
family means unity,
and he raised me to be
the woman I am.
We watched Disney movies
and bowled.
In his white tank top,
his muscles bulged.
It was his strength
that made me bold.

Denial.

I visited Ye Ye
before going off to school.
He greeted me
with his same soft eyes,
but it took him a while
to walk to my side.
His legs seemed to trail behind,
his head leading and
his shoulders hunched, misaligned.
His tank was looser
and his arms softer,
but I told Grandma
it was because he's older.
No need to worry,
Ye Ye and I had never been closer.

Anger.

The clues were there,
but I was too unaware,
focused on my future
and what I remembered
Ye Ye to be.
Stupid me.
My grandma noticed,
but we brushed it off
without a second glance.
How could I be this blind?

Bargaining.

If only we had known
it was Ye Ye's life that we
threw around
and that our loved ones
could get sick, too.
I just thought he couldn't do
the things we used to.
What I wouldn't give to be
that innocent
and play with Ye Ye
when he was strong
and could swing me
from his arms,
his little monkey.

Depression.

My second week of college.
That's when I found out
that his pancreas had cancer,
stage 4.
My world spun.
Could life be so evil
to take my best friend,

my role model?
My uneaten lunch sat there,
no longer appetizing.
My fingers wouldn't move,
I couldn't book a flight back home.
I ran up to my room,
    fell on my floor,
    unable to breathe.
People kept knocking on my door;
my sobbing, so loud,
alerted the whole dorm.
I tried to move from bed to floor
and back again,
but I couldn't move the sadness
away.
It was there to stay.
I tried to research the disease.
Those statistics
made me tremble,
the treatments, I'd learn,
would be painful.
There was no one around
I knew well enough—
I was alone.
And Ye Ye was far away,
back at home.

Acceptance.

Ye Ye and I talk every night,
even when seeing him
is painful.
I tell him with all my heart,
I love you.
I've grown more mature,
his granddaughter, his caretaker,
I remind him to take his pills

go to the doctor,
play cards rather than
monkey around.
Feigned optimism weighs on my back
instead of my class books
to bring him joy
when the sea of lost hope
begins to rise against him.
His appetite is gone.
Chemo steals his love
for food—
even more painful
since sharing a meal
is the Chinese way
of sharing love.
Our meals are now cooked
with time and hope,
the ingredients for acceptance.
I know the importance
of relationships,
of cherishing each moment
when the only constant
is change.
Ye Ye fights,
I grow,
and our love swells stronger.

Based off a story shared with author by Cristalle Choi

Diary of a Young Traveler:
A Second Moment in Morocco

This headscarf provided respite
from the heavy sun and sandy wind
as each step took us deeper into the Sahara.

My headscarf now rests peacefully,
as we face the sun's descent
with shadows snaking across the
floating sand—
barely making a sound—
mingling with my breaths
and the memories playing
in my mind.

So many strangers sitting by my side,
our feet resting just below the surface
in the cool sand,
yet I feel alone
trekking through
the thoughts in my head.

My life has been a blessing,
fulfilling, good.
I've come so far.

If my eyes closed
with the lowering sun,
and never opened again,
I would not be upset.
I would have no regrets,
only pride in what I've done
and where I've come from.

With my headscarf on,
my eyes resting,
I find full peace
with myself,
just like that day
floating in Ha-Long Bay.

Based off a story shared with author by Ching-Chi Tu

The Reason

Why, God, why?
When so many others have died?

I was passed out in the bathroom, alone.
But my friend heard,
and help was soon to come.
My body was red and itchy as
I fought for breath and
breath fought me.
It was then I learned
that food could be deadly.

In the ambulance, I asked for a priest
to bless me and the eggroll in my belly.
I was dying, but the medic said I'd be fine,
I would have to be careful what I ate next time—
I had a peanut allergy.

What has peanuts? What doesn't?
The freedom to eat had vanished.
Food filled me with fear,
anxiety, and confusion.
God, why'd You let me live?
There has to be a reason.
I mourned everything
I'd taken for granted.

I was set to go to Greece,
but on planes there's always
peanuts.
Anaphylactic shock on a transatlantic flight,
I couldn't take a risk like that.
I sent my friend without me,
the fear too consuming.

How am I supposed to live, God?
Why do I have to go through this?
God, why'd You let me live?

...

Thank you, God,
These two children of mine,
I don't have to raise them in fear.
Their allergies are more numerous
than the stars You promised Abraham.
You put me here to protect them.
I've finally learned Your reason.

Based off a story shared with author by Mary Bove

"I Do"

This was not how she expected her wedding night to go.
Her new husband hops across
the hood of their car,
screaming in fear as a feral dog
hops along, trying to grab a bite
of his tuxedo, black against white snow
that their car sits stuck in.
Maybe she should be upset
that their perfect night ended up like this,
but she is trying not to let him see her laugh,
as she curls up in the front seat like a roly poly, shaking
in her attempts at containing her glee.
Her new husband continues hopping
like a pogo stick, denting their car,
leaving this memory forever marked.

It's partly their fault they are here,
stuck in some stranger's yard,
fleeing from this crazy dog,
lost in the mountain snow.
Their reservations don't begin until tomorrow,
but they didn't see any harm in trying
for tonight (it's the time before cell phones),
and now here they are.
A stranger exits his large, resort-like house.
Her new husband sighs in relief,
finally someone to free him from the dog, from the snow,
a hero in a fancy robe.
The stranger looks at the car.
He looks at her husband and angrily says:
"DO NOT HIT MY TREE!"
As if they were just a minor inconvenience
to his wintry bliss,
he waltzes back inside,
his raging dog a ghost in his eyes.

Her new husband is flustered, panicked, and red,
and her laughter leaves her in stitches,
unable to help him.
He looks around at their situation:
his hopping, the dog's barking,
his wife's laughing, the car's sticking.
A look of insight fills his flushed face.
He sneakily pulls bark off the neighbor's beloved tree
and places it under the tires to build traction,
avoiding the dog and its sharp teeth's snapping.
It was not how she expected her wedding night to go,
but it made a memory to hold for years to come,
to cherish when they're old.

Based off a story shared with author by Patricia Bove

TV Screens and Love

The TV is flashing through the dark room
as it is known to do after the sun has set.
It is traveling through the windows silently,
the volume lowered slightly,
to mingle with the single streetlight
at the end of the front lawn.
A flickering image of peaceful moments easily forgotten.

Yet, this moment has a certain heaviness to it,
like a feather that a child finds
while he is out playing one morning
and decides to store it in his treasure box,
because he found value in it even after the bird let it drop.
Because inside this house, past the TV lights,
sits a man and his beautiful wife.

They aren't quite as young anymore,
both their children out of the house.
They've been married for a while,
and yet, until now,
they haven't spent much time as just themselves.
He looks at her, sitting attentive to their show,
thinks about how their life had gone.
They barely knew each other when they married,
and their daughter came a couple of years later.
Sometimes he was head over heels for her,
and sometimes she was for him.
Sometimes things were strong, sometimes the ice was thin.
He thought about the ups and downs and finally,
all she has done for them.

She came from a life of uncertainty,
she tried to balance a career

111

while being the one to rear their two beautiful children.
She pushed them in ways he never could:
like a flower needs to be watered,
but also needs the harsh sunlight to grow,
she nurtured and encouraged
until they had the confidence to bloom and go.
He realized that she was constantly giving,
even when her father died and she was mourning,
she strove to never let her children know
that she was hurting so,
and just hugged them a little tighter,
until she knew she had to let them go.

The colors of the TV screen vie for his attention,
but in that moment, he ignores them,
reflecting on how he had been gifted
with such an amazing woman as his wife;
he is where he is because of her—
sometimes he can take her for granted.
Her eyes are lit up, a beautiful brown,
in them he sees her soul, and all he can do is think:
oh, how much I love this woman in front of me.

Based off a story shared with author by Chris Bove

A Wish Upon a Star

Sometimes dreams really do come true,
like a fairy tale princess wishes them to
when she stares longingly at the stars.

In a college dorm, an enchanted castle, she sits
dreaming of *The Importance of Being Earnest*
and in it, the role she'd love to have.

But our princess doesn't just dream,
she works hard and practices the audition scene
until she knows she's ready to perform.

She is excited for the casting day,
any role, she knows, she'd be excited to play,
but she stifles any dream for the lead.

A few nights later, she jumps from her seat,
full of excitement and disbelief,
she's to portray her favorite role in her favorite show!

Questions run under her glistening crown,
she's a freshman, no experience, she doubts,
surely, there's someone better?

She's never seen herself as a princess
deserving of this role alongside her prince, Ernest.
Could she be Cecily, would she dare?

As she thinks about her dream and her dedication,
she reflects upon her practice and her passion.
She can play this role.

Our princess looks gratefully to the stars,
proud of the toil it took to get this far.
Sometimes dreams really do come true.

Based off a story shared with author by Kiersten Schutz

113

A Lesson in Humility

His prescription bottle
was a never-empty horn of plenty,
even when it should've been.
Those opioids were a crutch,
but we were blind, denying.

I was used to seeing addiction.
It was the nature of my work,
but I saw it from the outside.
It would never be my problem,
I was stupid, blind with pride.

On the day the USA
played Japan in women's soccer,
we found them,
hypodermic needles,
a second cornucopia.

Of course, he would stop
as long as we asked.
Hindsight is 20/20,
I guess.
Then the stealing started.

Lawnmowers, jewels,
TVs, computers disappearing,
remorse, forgiveness,
addiction, stealing,
again, cycling.

For him, each item was
the ticket to his next high.
He walked around the house

like an auditor evaluating prices,
figuring out what to sell in order to buy.

When the phone rang,
my heart would stop.
I felt so lost—
how had we fallen so far?
My pride, at rock bottom, curled into a ball.

I had to stand in line,
waiting to see my son,
wondering what he had done.
The jailtime blues a constant
melody in my head, hopeless.

My denial enabled
his horn of plenty.
We were searching for answers.
We needed help.
He couldn't stay here anymore.

Were we sending him to his death,
away from stability, family?
The fear held our hearts,
but we could no longer be still.
Staying here could kill him, too.

We moved him to
a sober-living home.
he said he was committed.
There were setbacks,
but he did his best, staying clean.

He got a job,
an apartment,

115

a college degree,
a girlfriend.
She got pregnant.

I was scared,
but he held it together,
and that April evening,
as I looked at his beautiful baby,
I felt peace.

He named the baby after me,
a way of saying thanks
for the first time—
for pushing him,
for emptying his cornucopia.

Tonight, as I reflect,
he's eight years sober.
We are blessed.
His story is not over,
and today is a good day.

I had to have this lesson
in humility,
to realize my dreams for him
are mine, not his.
He's alive, he's free.

The pride I held in
those I work with is gone.
In its place, more compassion,
more connection.
Above all, I'm proud of my son.

——————————————

Based off a story shared with author by an anonymous source

Coloring Book Arms

The flashing of my feet in my light–up sneaks
matches the flashing of the pretty window signs,
look how it goes: *red, blue, white, blue, red, red, white.*
I want to look closer at the lights.
My feet move faster, I'm skipping forward!

I see three boys, lit up by signs,
they look so strong with their coloring book arms.
I bet they could carry all my toys!
I want to ask about the pictures on their skin.
My feet move faster, I'm skipping forward!

Until Daddy yanks my arm backwards, I almost fall.
I stomp my foot and want to cry *Daddy, let me see the lights!*
He looks me in the eye and tells me to look again:
I see a little boy, pulled back by his mommy,
shielding her son from the coloring book boys.

I'm starting to see a whole new world.
The flashing sign is so bright:
it hurts, burns my eyes!
Ouch, make it stop, I don't want to see the lights.
My feet shuffle behind my daddy, save me, save me!

Three scary men, not boys, wear fake grins
with razor sharp teeth, like sharks in the sea.
Their arms covered in pictures of monsters,
I want to run away from them.
My feet shuffle behind my daddy, save me, save me!

Until Daddy hugs me strong, tightly, I melt in his arms.
I close my eyes, want to cry, *Daddy, keep me safe tonight!*
He looks me in the eyes and holds my hand,

*I'll protect you from the scary men and remember:
what you see isn't always what you get.*

Based off a story shared with author by Sara C.

The Perfume of Hope

My stepdad got a job
as a doorman in Manhattan,
so we picked up our lives
and moved to the projects.

I was a freshman thinking,
I'm too old to make new friends,
high school will be terrible,
as I stared forlornly out the window.

From the sixteenth floor,
I had a decent view
of poverty but also hope—
a perfume for the stench of despair.

As I was spiraling in my brain,
a swirl of smoke danced
on the other side of the glass,
gray, like sky muted by city lights.

I was entranced and then realized,
Oh, there's a fire!
What can I do,
what if there're people in there?

I ran down the stairs,
panting, concerned,
banged on the door,
hoping the renter heard.

I was screaming, shouting,
knocking, pounding,
and finally, a boy, big as a thimble,
opened the door, confused at my babble.

I looked at him and said,
there's a fire, you have to get out!
But he didn't budge,
his little brother was inside.

Where's your dad? I asked.
Sleeping, he was sleeping.
I pushed past the boy
and again, started screaming.

The father came out,
tired from the night shift.
to a fire in the kitchen
from the little boy's cooking.

I got the boys out,
the father tackled the fire,
and a little while later,
the firemen had it handled.

Ten years later, another tragedy:
the little brother had died,
fallen from the window, high
on cocaine, addicted.

Even in their pain, hope seeped
through burning curtains, out of
the little brother's open window,
a rotten perfume masking fire, death, despair.

Why was life in the projects like this?
How could hope prevail amid flames?
It somehow did, and thank God,
my life is better for it.

———————————————————

Based off a story shared with author by Olga Repp

Symphony of Light

scrreeee- **phooo**
the bus jolts to a stop in front of the small camp.
a scramble of kids jumps off the cramped steps,
excited to break from the monotony of school.
then they stop in confusion when they see the lake,
it looked like they wouldn't get to swim after all, it was a little too small.

*shhaa***shh**
leaves come alive as wind wakes to setting sun,
a new quiet comes over the camp. counselors corral students
one by one, flashlights on, and a line of light bobs towards the beach.
almost as quickly, the lights extinguish as
the children lay their heads on the rough sand.

*heee-***chrrr-***heeeeh-***chrsshh**
waves whipping the shore accompany their muffled breaths,
permeate the silence. the students peer at the vacuum of pitch black,
speckled with twinkling stars that seem so far, glimmering,
every blank space filled, and every few seconds, streaks of white run across the sky
with the same fiery energy of the scrambling kids.

*bmmmp-***bmmmp**
emily's heart slows to a crawl as she feels the weight
of the universe, the presence of all the other students.
she feels small as a grain of sand beneath her head—
not worthless, but power in the vastness, awe and humility,
grounded in life's grandness.

Based off a story shared with author by Emily VanderBent

121

Cold Front

The news of a storm,
the air full of specks of snow
shut down the airport;
there was no way to go.
They had prepped for weeks,
to travel to DC,
to march for life, to do
what they believed right.

She wouldn't be silenced.
She had to be there.
It was a God-given right,
her duty.
She called the airport,
but no flights were leaving,
she called the local university,
but she was only seventeen—
too young, they said,
to take the journey.

So she called Amtrak,
bought a single ticket,
to go alone.
The night of the trip,
the drive to the station
was met with hydroplaning
on black ice.
The train was delayed,
and next to her, a creepy guy,
who winked and said,
 "wake me up when the train arrives."

A bmp ch bmp a bmp ch
The slight jostling of the train cars

kept time like a broken clock.
The journey long, especially
in coach, alone, the wintry night air
running in as the doors opened
with each stop.
She sat in her seat, scared,
hoping the Virgin Mary was there
with a veil to wrap them both—
two teenage girls,
traveling into the unknown.

Two hours later,
as the doors opened once more,
warmth mingled with the cool air
as one of her friends boarded the train.
Her friend came with a family,
a welcome sight for this lonely girl.
She moved to their seats,
no longer in coach,
and pretended to be asleep
whenever the conductor approached.

This journey was worth it,
she had made the effort, and
change was in the air.
She did all she could
to show she cared,
and let the truth slice
through the cold, dark night.

Based off a story shared with author by Teresa Muñoz

Passing Trains

With the setting sun, the goodbyes come,
and this one is forever.
Off he goes, from one college to another.
He makes his rounds, hugs abound,
up two floors to a girl next door,
he tells her straight, without delay:
"I'm leaving this place."
When she asks why, he cannot lie,
just as he can't deny the mountains' call—
if only his friends could come, too.

Then he knows, 'fore the moment is through,
this will stick with him like glue.
Our girl next door begins to bawl,
he sits concerned, losing control.
Her strong heart crawls out her chest,
at her speaking mouth's behest
with an avalanche of private words.
He formulates a responding herd.
With no reason to dive, deeper they go.
If they'll see each other again, they really don't know,
but with their stories, they briefly connect,
it is here their lives intersect.

Like two sole passengers awake in two trains,
full steam ahead in opposing lanes,
with the glimmer of lamps as their only light,
with nothing to fear but the darkness of night,
they look outside to try to find something besides
their reflection, their lonely lives.
Passing, connecting, for a simple stare,
their lives, forever, together ensnared.

How simple it is to open and share,
with someone, a stranger, who surprisingly
cares.

Based off a story shared with author by an anonymous source

The Punching Bag Ghosts

*This poem contains topics that may be sensitive for some readers. *

Once a week, Coach Bove
would teach kickboxing
at the local YMCA,
sometimes it was tiring,
but she rarely complained.
She loved what she did
(never mind not earning a living wage).
She'd see familiar faces
make healthy life changes,
seek outlets for their frustrations.

One night, as the punching bags were swinging
(making it seem like ghosts were
running around the room,
snaking between them,
playing tag),
class was over
and she prepared to leave,
one student stayed back,
wanting to talk with her coach
before the gym lights turned off,
the ghosts stopped playing,
and the magic of the moment had passed.

This student was a regular,
each week she'd come,
quiet but capable, determined
to get her workout done.
This week was no exception,
so what sparked this conversation?

The student began to talk,
thanking the coach for all her hard work,

she loved the class,
but this week might be her last.
The class was her outlet,
each week she could come,
and hear Coach Bove tell her she was strong.

She would feel empowered, confident,
for this hour each week,
and then she'd go home.

Her boyfriend didn't think her strong.
He abused her.
She felt weak.
She didn't have the courage to leave.
All she could do was
kickbox once a week
where she felt seen,
and could depend on her own power.
And today, she could finally say
she was ready to leave,
to fight for herself, to move—
and now she knew,
she'd be okay, she was brave.
And that's why today
would be her last day.

The coach fought back quiet tears,
even the ghosts stopped playing,
amazed, listening.

Coach Bove was stunned—
she did what she loved
provided an outlet,
but didn't expect this class
to give such hope,
to have such impact.

Everything was worth it,
and moving forward,
no hard day at the gym could
dampen her purpose.

They haven't seen each other since,
but the punching bag ghosts
watch over the student
wherever she may go.
And as for the coach,
every time she walks in a gym,
the ghosts make way,
and they pause their play,
to honor how important
her work is.

Based off a story shared with author by Marcya Bove

The Performance of a Lifetime

Rewind three years to when the bell rang,
a death march mixed with high school twang,
just a kid singing with his friends,
with hopes to become something,
to change the world, to light the stage.
Teenage dreams with endless roads ahead,
until a detour, cancer,
growing uncontrollably.
Not much to do but pray
and fight, keep fighting.
The bell clamors to be heard,
but songs still have the power of words
that drown out the fear and the pain,
and he still strives.

A couple of months later,
at the Ryman, it's a big night.
With his doctor by his side,
he'll fight another time,
singing for an adoring crowd—
finding his voice—
his love and his dream,
makes him
normal, and unique.
His road is clearer, the path direct,
but the detour shortened the distance.
Time is of the essence,
not much to do but pray
and fight, keep fighting,
together they sing.
All lights on him, all light from him,
the joy he has in pain, inspiring.

And then he speaks
over the infamous melody
of bells.
Who could not listen to a
kid with such a malady, when
there's not much to do, but pray
and fight, keep fighting?

He knows, this is not what he planned,
we can't always choose what happens to us
but we can choose how we respond:
we can let the bells march us into darkness,
or when the world is in their shadow,
we can be the light,
and trust, and fight, and pray that
tomorrow will be a brand new, sunny day.

Raymond M. Cruz. "First Time Performing At The Ryman !." August 11, 2018.
Video, 6:23
"We can't always choose what happens to us, but we can choose how we
respond" is a direct quote
Learn more about Raymond Cruz's story at https://www.rayoflighttn.com/

The Hummingbird's Wings,
Stronger than the Demons' Screams

This poem contains topics that may be sensitive for some readers.

His love for hummingbirds
started when we were young,
his way of coping, the power
in their tiny wings, enticing.
I loved their freedom to fly,
so I followed, leaving all I knew
for the nectar of the world,
leaving home, leaving Alan alone.

He tried to go, too,
but he kept getting pulled back down.
He poured bitter drinks,
hoping to swim out of the hole
that his despair, his fear had dug.

He fed the hummingbirds,
the beating of their wings,
helps the beating of his heart,
giving him strength—
we prayed, he tried.

One night, the demons called
from their hole,
hummingbirds in torpor, sleeping.
For a moment, he was weak.
His soul flew from his body.

The next morning, my heart heavy,
cool air the only solace
to my numbness.
As I allowed myself to wonder about

131

a world without Alan,
a hummingbird's chatter interrupts
in the middle of September—
I hadn't seen one all summer.

Alan's demons, that night, may have won,
but the next morning,
the demons were no match for the hummingbird's thrum.
Alan may have felt small,
but his wings, I know,
have always been so strong.

Based off a story shared with author by Kasey Ginn

An Ode to Leila

Comic books sit unread, fading
as new heroes dot the horizon like giants
covered in face masks, contaminated.
Doctors, nurses thanked daily; companies make their PPE.
Stethoscopes, not capes, guard the night from viral villains,
making things right. Sacrifice, pain, fatigue.
New statues will rise through home sewing.
So deserving, shout thanks from the rooftops.
But these heroes stand by, lost among the ranks,
expecting nothing.

Here rests Leila, the first of many,
as her coworkers keep fighting, daily,
odds against them greatly.
One doctor, nurse, sick for every nineteen in their charge.
The patients aren't the only ones behind bars.
Every day, a death march, one step closer,
as the air provides sweet oxygen tainted with odors
of illness, fear. Forty dollars for an eighty-cent gown—
The price of protection. Who makes their PPE?
They are serving the least of these.

In good times, unsung. In bad, forgotten.
Leila and the others, doctors, nurses,
like trees fighting to survive on mountains,
without enough clean air to share,
but providing shade and shelter.
Inevitable suffering. Inevitable hope.
These are the heroes whose memories we must hold.
Remember Leila, her life, her love.
Remember their sacrifice, pain, fatigue.
Remember everything.

Based off a story shared with author by Jorge Dominicis

To My Younger Self

Dear me,
Oh, how weird that is to say.
I feel a little bit like a child
with my dreams and musings,
like when I used to sign my diary:
TTYL, Love ME :)
But *dear me,* these are things
that I wish I had said
long before my twenties
or even my teens,
before anxiety sat
at the top of the stairs, its
claws on the banister, its
head leaned over the edge,
grabbing my thoughts as they floated
from my mind, twisting them into lies:
    "You can't do it, you're not good enough.
Don't bother asking for help,
you'll just be judged."

Dear me,
it's okay to ask for help,
don't wait until rock bottom,
worries high, no job in sight.
The worst they can say is no,
and a no won't make now any worse.
Ask for help, let others ask you.
Struggle together,
it is through this that we grow.
Take these lessons, dear me,
and hold them tight,
they will help you—me—
in life.

Based off a story shared with author by Michelle Tran

that we may know and, therefore, love.

ACKNOWLEDGMENTS

———

Writing this book has been a dream come true. When I struggled with doubts about my talent or ability to write an entire book, I reflected on the bottom of the bookshelf in my childhood room. This shelf contained neatly stacked, torn, wide-lined notebooks full of book ideas and starting chapters, and the hope of my inner child pushed me to continue writing. That said, I would not be able to reflect on the satisfaction of accomplishing my childhood goal without acknowledging so many important, caring people. Without their help, A Day of Humanity would not have been possible.

First, I am so grateful to my family, especially my parents, Chris and Marcya Bove, who have always pushed me to follow my passions; as my mom always says, "Do your best and forget the rest." Thank you to my brother, Davis Bove, for your patient love in this process and by motivating me with poetry.

Thank you to Alejandro Muñoz for all of your support—for listening to me read my book aloud for hours and for providing constructive notes.

Thank you to every single person who shared their stories with me and allowed me to work them into poems of connection and humanity. Quite literally, there would be no book without you.

Thank you to everyone who supported me through kind words and encouragement as I enthusiastically discussed my book at any possible moment.

A huge thanks to Professor Eric Koester and Brian Bies for leading me into this wonderful world of book writing, to Elissa Graeser, Lisa Patterson, Bailee Noella, and Kara Cochran for being incredible editors, and to my publisher, New Degree Press, for making this book a reality.

This book was partly inspired by my faith and the connections I receive from it, so I would like to thank my God for the gift of writing and the inspiration to share His love.

Finally, thank you to all those who pre-ordered and donated to A Day of Humanity to push me closer to my dream. I am sincerely grateful for all of your help.

Dan Gilbert

Christopher Bove

Sara Crozier

Leilani Boulware

Lindsey Kimery

Olga Repp

Andrew D Walter

Elisia Hamm

Jennifer Elzweig

Elias J Calisto

Patricia Bove

Edwin Vazquez

Haley Newlin

Christopher Larkins

Shawn, Cherie, and Jaxton Carter

Kevin Stout

Janece Shaffer

Tricia Thiesing

Eric Koester

J. A. Muñoz

Mary Elizabeth Blakeney Kehler

Andrew Lewis

Kendra Rider

The Cherry Hill Boves

Chris and Maggie Rolince

Healey Sample

Cristi Bell-Huff

Braden Cole

Shelby Lauren Hash

Thomas Mogish

Teri Levy

Sarah Thomas, JD

Toni Seibert

Brice Maurice

Jared Brown

Lisa Jass

Hillary Gold

Lily Turaski

Rosa M Acosta

Angel Asirvatham

Jen Ternullo

Lily Gao

Jonathan Stout

Noah Pilz

Ellen B. Donnelly

Kegan Dellinger

Ehsan Maleki

Teresa Muñoz

Zach Donahue

Natalie Pacitto

Kasia Kwasniak

Zain Raza

Davis Bove

Marcya Bove

Lauren Nichols

Nikolina Kosanovic

Jesse Eli Franklin

Kasey Ginn

Hill Duggan

Morten Bove

Caroline Nannis

Kaitlyn Stout

Margarita Muñoz

Joe Dunlop

Sophie Hill

Kathy Cabezas

Alicia Robang

Graham Ward Lovell

Marc Papas

Godwin Chan

Timothy Wu

Brenda Morris

Carlos Najera

Andrew Elam

Erika Ceyssens

APPENDIX

———

AUTHOR'S NOTE

Frost, Robert. "The Road Not Taken," *Poetry Foundation*.
Accessed on June 1, 2020.
https://www.poetryfoundation.org/poems/44272/
the-road-not-taken

Polack, Ellie. "New Cigna Study Reveals Loneliness at
Epidemic Levels in America." Cigna. May 1, 2018.
https://www.cigna.com/newsroom/news-
releases/2018/new-cigna-study-reveals-loneliness-
at-epidemic-levels-in-america

TENNESSEE'S AUBREY NOT KANSAS' DOROTHY

Beres, Nick. "In The Face of Such Devastation . . . And,
The Loss of 25 Lives You Try to Look For Small
Silver Linings," Facebook, Last Modified March 3,
2020.
https://www.facebook.com/NickBeresNC5/photos/
a.10151994787066640/10156771352971640/?type
=3&theater

NICKIE.

Reilly, Matthew. Scarecrow: A Shane Schofield Thriller.
London: St. Martin's Press, 2004.

THE PERFORMANCE OF A LIFETIME

Raymond M. Cruz. "First Time Performing At The
Ryman!." August 11, 2018. Video, 6:23.
https://youtu.be/7CU0hmw4Hu0.

ABOUT THE AUTHOR

Brady Bove is a true believer in the beauty of humanity with an innate desire to understand the world. Her engineering background combined with her passion for poetry allows her to meld the mechanics and the emotions of life. Bove's empathetic nature not only gives her the strength to cry at sad movies but to draw on the experiences of others to highlight the intricacies of human nature through the emotions and experiences that connect us all. Her love of hiking and traveling, spending time with her family, and diving into her Catholic faith fuel her view of the world and deepen her connection with those in it.

Made in the USA
Columbia, SC
10 August 2020